A PARRAGON BOOK
Published by Parragon Books, Unit 13-17 Avonbridge Trading Estate,
Atlantic Road, Avonmouth, Bristol BS11 9QD
Produced by The Templar Company plc, Pippbrook Mill,
London Road, Dorking, Surrey RH4 1JE
Copyright © 1994 Parragon Book Service Limited
All rights reserved
Designed by Janie Louise Hunt
Edited by Caroline Steeden
Printed and bound in Italy
ISBN 1-85813-951-1

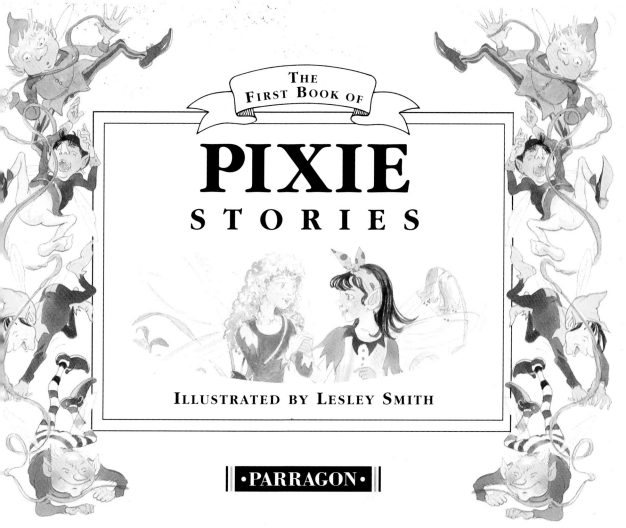

THE FIRST BOOK OF

PIXIE

STORIES

ILLUSTRATED BY LESLEY SMITH

·PARRAGON·

This Book
Belongs to

N   Grace hake

*13 oak Lands Ave

west wickNHam

ken te 98 zI

07817 79

CONTENTS

A WISH TOO FAR

WRITTEN BY DAVE KING

Nathan was bored. He wasn't just bored in that "Ho Hum! I haven't got a thing to do!" kind of way that most of us feel every now and then. Oh no, he was bored in a full blown, major league, top of the list, wet Sunday afternoon in a boring seaside town kind of way, that makes you pace around for an hour and a half before screaming, "IIIIII'm boooorrred!!" at the top of your voice.

Strangely enough, it was a wet Sunday afternoon in a boring seaside town. Nathan's parents had brought him

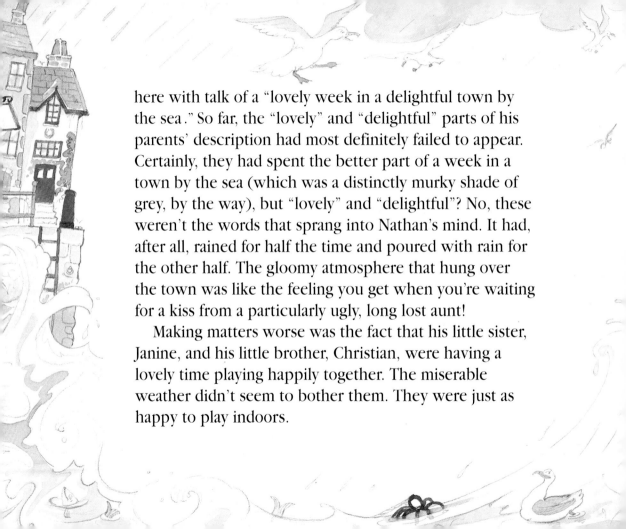

here with talk of a "lovely week in a delightful town by the sea." So far, the "lovely" and "delightful" parts of his parents' description had most definitely failed to appear. Certainly, they had spent the better part of a week in a town by the sea (which was a distinctly murky shade of grey, by the way), but "lovely" and "delightful"? No, these weren't the words that sprang into Nathan's mind. It had, after all, rained for half the time and poured with rain for the other half. The gloomy atmosphere that hung over the town was like the feeling you get when you're waiting for a kiss from a particularly ugly, long lost aunt!

Making matters worse was the fact that his little sister, Janine, and his little brother, Christian, were having a lovely time playing happily together. The miserable weather didn't seem to bother them. They were just as happy to play indoors.

Nathan just wanted the holiday to be over and to get back home. Unfortunately, they still had another two days to go. Nathan paced up and down, sat grumpily in a chair (ignoring the book that his dad had bought for him), or sat in front of the television, flicking between the channels. And still the rain pitter-pattered against the window.

"I wish I could be on my own somewhere, without my family getting under my feet!" he thought, gloomily.

Finally, he got up and grabbed his coat. "Where are you going?" asked his mum.

"Into the garden!" he replied.

His mum sighed wearily. "But it's still raining!"

Nathan put on his coat.

"I don't care!" he said. "I'm going to stand in the garden and grow roots and become a tree and then I'll be stuck here for ever!" And with that, he stomped out.

"Cor!" said Janine, excitedly. "That sounds brilliant! Come on, Chris, let's go and watch!"

Out in the garden, Nathan splashed across the muddy grass with his sister and brother following closely behind. As they neared the far end of the garden, Nathan turned to the others and began to snarl at them, continuing to walk backwards as he did so.

"Why don't you leave me alone?" he snapped.

"We want to see you turn into a tree!" Christian replied.

"Ohhh… that's all I need…" Nathan began, but was cut off as he disappeared from sight. Janine and Christian stopped in their tracks.

They looked down and saw a hole in the ground where Nathan had been walking. Peering down into it, they jumped back with shock as Nathan's head popped up.

"Aaaaahhhh!" they screamed in unison.

"It's okay!" replied Nathan. "The hole wasn't very deep! And look what I found down there…"

Nathan held up a small, shiny box that gleamed and sparkled, even in the gloomy rain.

"What is it?" Janine asked.

Just as she spoke, the box slipped from Nathan's fingers and landed on the wet grass. The lid flipped open and a twinkly swirl of light flew into the air. The children gasped in amazement, as a tiny figure materialised in front of them. A man, no more than five or six inches tall, hovered in the air before landing on a nearby sunflower. He had a bushy white beard and was wearing a pointed red hat.

15

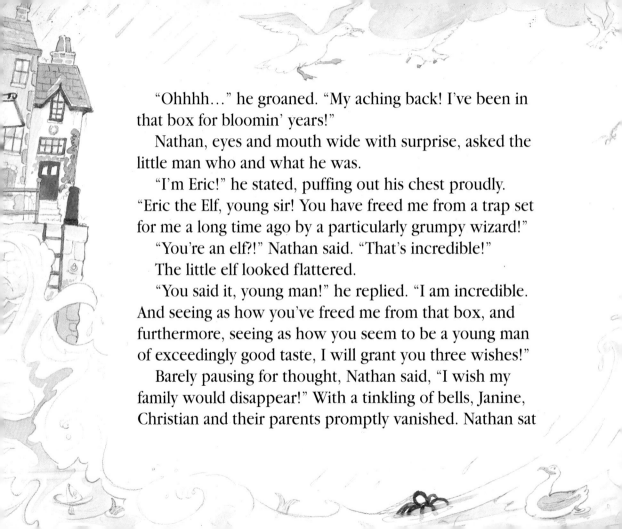

"Ohhhh…" he groaned. "My aching back! I've been in that box for bloomin' years!"

Nathan, eyes and mouth wide with surprise, asked the little man who and what he was.

"I'm Eric!" he stated, puffing out his chest proudly. "Eric the Elf, young sir! You have freed me from a trap set for me a long time ago by a particularly grumpy wizard!"

"You're an elf?!" Nathan said. "That's incredible!"

The little elf looked flattered.

"You said it, young man!" he replied. "I am incredible. And seeing as how you've freed me from that box, and furthermore, seeing as how you seem to be a young man of exceedingly good taste, I will grant you three wishes!"

Barely pausing for thought, Nathan said, "I wish my family would disappear!" With a tinkling of bells, Janine, Christian and their parents promptly vanished. Nathan sat on the wet grass, not quite believing what had happened.

"Is… is that it?" he asked. "Are they r…really gone?"

Eric gestured around the garden. "Look around you !" he said. Certainly, Janine and Christian were no longer there. Eric leant forwards and prodded Nathan. "Listen, sonny, I'm a busy elf! What's your second wish?"

"I wish I was somewhere nice and hot, all by myself!" Nathan answered. And suddenly, he was alone on a beautiful beach, the blue sky arching high over his head and the sea glittering like polished diamonds and stretching away for ever.

"Wow!" Nathan said, getting to his feet and running across the hot sand. "This is brilliant, eh, Eric? Eric?" There was no answer. Nathan whirled around quickly, looking everywhere. "Eric?" he shouted again, but there was no reply, only the sound of the sea, lapping gently at the shore.

He ran around for what seemed like ages, but the empty beach seemed to have no end, and the tropical forest that bordered the beach looked a bit dark and scary.

Finally, hot, tired and more than a little worried, he flopped down on the sand and began to sob quietly. If only he could be back with all his family around him in that funny little bungalow on the edge of the wet and dreary seaside town!

"Well, I'm sure that can be arranged!" said a little voice at Nathan's side, making him jump. It was Eric. "You said you wanted to be alone, so I thought I'd give you a little time to yourself!"

"I want to go back and I want my family to be back with me!" Nathan said, breathlessly.

"And is that your third and final wish, then?" Eric asked. Nathan nodded his head vigorously.

"Oh, it is! It is!" he said.

"I'll see what I can do," said Eric.

19

Janine tugged at his arm and Nathan felt the rain against his face. "Come up out of that hole!" she said, as she and Christian peered down at him. Nathan climbed out of the damp hole and looked around, feeling very glad to be back. He could see his mum and dad inside the house and thought to himself that it was one of the nicest sights he had ever seen.

"Your brother and sister won't remember me!" Eric said, appearing in front of Nathan. "But I think you will, and you'll remember what you learnt today!"

"You bet!" Nathan said. "I'll never take my family for granted again! Even if they do bring me for a lovely week in a delightful town by the sea!"

And as Eric twinkled from sight, Nathan looked up at the grey sky, took his sister's hand, and ran inside laughing to join his family!

PUFFCHEEK'S PALACE

WRITTEN BY GEOFF COWAN

If you walk carefully and quietly through a woodland dell, don't be startled to hear faint voices and glimpse some colourfully dressed little people. For there may be elves and pixies about, just like there were in the woods behind the garden of Kate's cottage home. Only, her brother Sam didn't believe her. Then something very strange happened that made him begin to wonder…

"Pull!" cried Topknot, sitting grandly on a small carriage he had found while going early-morning exploring.

He had fetched the other elves, and they were using a rope of woven grass to tow his discovery away. However, nothing much happened in those woods without the sharp-eyed pixies noticing. When they saw the carriage, they wanted to join in the fun.

"Push!" shouted Puffcheek to his fellow pixies.

So the elves pulled the carriage while the pixies pushed, until it lurched and Topknot almost fell off.

"Pulling's safer than pushing me along!" he called, grumpily.

"But pushing's easier, especially if you go downhill!" protested Puffcheek. "Watch! We'll show you!"

Before Topknot could stop them, Puffcheek and the other pixies gave such a mighty shove that the carriage suddenly sped forward. It moved so fast that the startled elves hardly had time to jump out of the way.

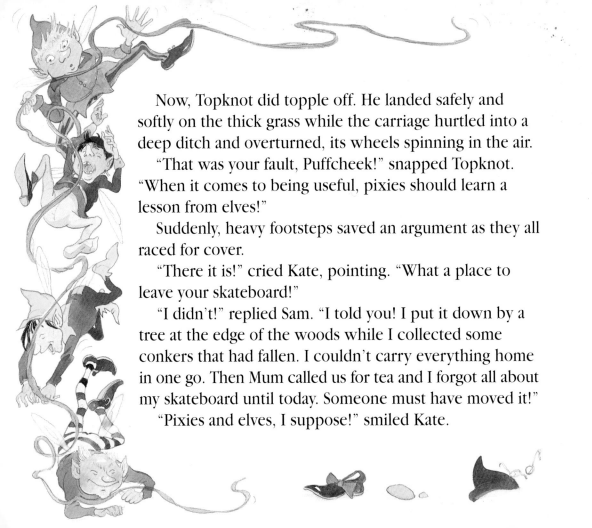

Now, Topknot did topple off. He landed safely and softly on the thick grass while the carriage hurtled into a deep ditch and overturned, its wheels spinning in the air.

"That was your fault, Puffcheek!" snapped Topknot. "When it comes to being useful, pixies should learn a lesson from elves!"

Suddenly, heavy footsteps saved an argument as they all raced for cover.

"There it is!" cried Kate, pointing. "What a place to leave your skateboard!"

"I didn't!" replied Sam. "I told you! I put it down by a tree at the edge of the woods while I collected some conkers that had fallen. I couldn't carry everything home in one go. Then Mum called us for tea and I forgot all about my skateboard until today. Someone must have moved it!"

"Pixies and elves, I suppose!" smiled Kate.

Sam laughed and scrambled into the ditch. He picked up his skateboard, then headed for home. Kate was about to follow when she spotted the elves' grass rope that had broken free from the skateboard. Kate looked at it thoughtfully and put it in her pocket.

"So that's where the carriage came from," said Topknot, afterwards.

"You mean skateboard," corrected Puffcheek. "The Big People use all kinds of odd things and give them some very funny names!"

"Well, whatever they call it, I want it back!" cried Topknot. "Finders keepers. That's only fair!"

Even the pixies agreed, so Puffcheek had no choice but to try and recover the skateboard.

Which brought him to Kate's cottage garden. Sam had already gone to meet a friend, taking the skateboard with him. Meanwhile, Kate sat at the far end of the garden to examine the little grass rope. Puffcheek crept closer, searching for the skateboard. Suddenly, Kate sneezed and blew the pixie off a log he had clambered on to.

"Hey! Look out, clumsy!" he yelled and Kate was just close enough to hear.

"Oh, there really are pixies," she cried. "Did you make this rope!"

"No, it was the elves!" replied Puffcheek, picking himself up.

Then he remembered how much larger Big People were and was about to hurry away. It was only the thought of facing an angry Topknot without the skateboard that stopped him.

"I'll weave you a grass bracelet if you give me that carriage, er, skateboard," said Puffcheek.

"I was right! You did move it!" said Kate. "But the skateboard's not mine!"

Puffcheek explained what had happened. Then he sighed, "I can't return empty-handed to Topknot!"

Kate remembered something and had an idea. "Come back as the sun goes down and I may be able to help!"

Unbeknown to Kate, Sam had arrived home and come into the garden.

"Who were you talking to?" he asked Kate, puzzled.

"Oh, just a pixie!" she replied, playfully.

"You know you tidied up your cupboard yesterday. Didn't you say you wanted to get rid of your toy castle?" Kate asked.

Sam nodded. "I'm too big for it now!"

"I know someone who's just the right size!" said Kate. "Can I have it?"

"If you like," said Sam.

When Sam went inside, Kate fetched the little castle, complete with its turrets, drawbridge and battlements. She took it to the edge of the wood. At dusk, Puffcheek found the castle with a note from Kate telling him it was for Topknot.

"I'm sorry I was cross with you, Puffcheek!" said Topknot as, this time, the elves and pixies happily pushed and pulled the toy castle deeper into the woods. "A castle's better than a carriage any day!"

"You can call it 'Topknot's Castle'," said Puffcheek.
"Or 'Puffcheek's Palace'," replied Topknot kindly.
"It's yours as long as we can play inside and
have parties there! After all,
you were very brave to
speak to one of the
Big People!"

Puffcheek smiled proudly as the elves and pixies congratulated him.

Next morning, before school, Sam followed his sister into the garden.

"I saw you carrying my castle down to the bottom of the garden last night," he said. "You wanted to play with it yourself all along, didn't you?"

"No, I left it here," replied Kate, pointing. "But it's gone!"

"Just like my skateboard," said Sam, thoughtfully. "Shall we search for it?"

"No," replied Kate, who was very pleased to have helped Puffcheek and the others.

"Don't tell me you think the elves and pixies took my old toy castle too!" grinned Sam.

Kate nodded. "Who else?" she smiled. "Only, this time, I think we'll let them keep it!"

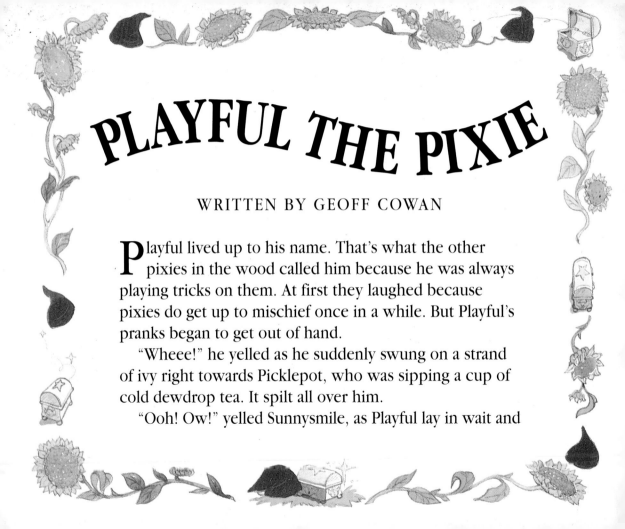

PLAYFUL THE PIXIE

WRITTEN BY GEOFF COWAN

Playful lived up to his name. That's what the other pixies in the wood called him because he was always playing tricks on them. At first they laughed because pixies do get up to mischief once in a while. But Playful's pranks began to get out of hand.

"Wheee!" he yelled as he suddenly swung on a strand of ivy right towards Picklepot, who was sipping a cup of cold dewdrop tea. It spilt all over him.

"Ooh! Ow!" yelled Sunnysmile, as Playful lay in wait and

pelted him with berries. The juice stained Sunnysmile's clothes.

"Grrrgh!" spluttered an unsuspecting Curlytoes when he pulled on his hat and found Playful had filled it with water. Truth was, the pixies were more than a little tired of Playful's non-stop naughtiness. Time and again they asked him to behave.

"A joke's a joke but you've gone too far, Playful," they warned.

"Or not far enough!" grumbled some. "Keep this up and you can go and play in someone else's patch of wood!"

Which is exactly what Playful did. One morning, he climbed out of bed extra early and set off across the meadow into another wood where a band of elves lived. And what a dance he led them, too. Playful made sure he kept himself hidden and puffed pollen on the elves to make them sneeze. While they slept, he swapped their boots around so they didn't fit!

"This is better fun than before," giggled Playful. "Now no one even knows it's me!"

That was until the elves caught him, for elves are much more clever than you might think. They knew someone had to be behind all the odd goings-on, so they laid a trap.

Playful fell for it; or it fell for Playful, to be exact. A carefully placed bag of honey dropped on his hat, bursting open, the next time he tried to creep up on the elves.

"Caught you!" they cried, feeling extremely pleased with themselves as they danced around a very gooey Playful.

"Mess with us and you'll come unstuck!" warned an elf named Echo. He was called Echo because he liked the sound of his own voice.

"I'm in a mess and all stuck up!" cried Playful, miserably.

"Serves you right!" sang Echo. "When you're washed and clean, we'll take you back where you came from."

One of the elves had guessed Playful was from The Other Wood because he'd heard it was full of pixies. When both bands came face to face, the pixies were startled to see Playful with the elves. They weren't so surprised to hear about all the bother he'd caused.

"The least we can do is invite you to a Pixie Party," Picklepot told the elves. "There'll be music, dancing and all the pixie pizzas you can eat!"

And more of Playful's pranks. The fact was he just couldn't seem to help himself. He sprinkled mud on the mushroom seats to make folk sit down with a squelch! He put jelly in a flower-trumpet so wobbly bits were blown out everywhere when the pixie band played; and that was only the start. The elves and pixies were fed up before they'd even eaten anything! When they did sit down to eat they were furious to discover that someone had mixed up all the food and put mustard in the jam sandwiches and tomato ketchup in the sponge cake. Things had gone beyond a joke!

It called for quick thinking before tempers flared. Picklepot and Echo drew up a plan. The first part was easy. For the rest of the party, the elves and pixies would take it in turns to watch Playful very carefully. If he showed the slightest sign of mischief, they would step in and stop him. The second part was harder…

Next morning, when Playful woke, what do you think his first thought of the day was? Which new tricks he should try out, of course! But he never got the chance to play any tricks, because he realised with a terrible shock that he had no idea where he was. And even worse, he was all alone. He was in a part of the wood he had never been to before.

43

"Trembling toadstools! Where am I?" gasped Playful, sitting up with a start. "Where is everyone?"

Before Playful could throw back his patchwork blanket, it flew off as if by magic, leaving him lying in his night-shirt.

"What's happening?" gasped Playful, reaching for the folded green tunic on the end of the bed. He went to pull it on and found he couldn't. It was much too tiny!

"Hey! That's not mine!" he cried, crossly.

At least the boots fitted but these weren't his either and they had big holes in the soles. Next moment, Playful spotted a folded piece of paper on the ground. His name was written on it in large letters. As Playful hurried to pick it up, the paper danced into the air then settled close by.

Playful hoped there might be a map on the other side to show him the way home. But every time he neared the paper, it fluttered further away until it landed long enough for Playful to pounce. Whoosh! A net hidden under some leaves sprang up and closed around him. Playful was whisked off his feet and found himself dangling in mid-air.

"Caught you!" cried a voice as Playful struggled.

"Let me down, whoever you are! Please stop playing tricks on me!" he called, dizzily. He was really rather frightened indeed.

"Only if you stop playing them on all of us!" said Picklepot, who stepped out from behind a tree with the other pixies.

"And us! And us!" repeated Echo who appeared with the elves.

"Yes! I promise!" said Playful, who was relieved to see them. They gently lowered the net and helped him out.

Now Playful noticed Sunnysmile holding the bed blanket tied to a long thread that he had used to pull it away. Another was tied to the note Playful had chased to lure him to the net. Curlytoes happily handed over Playful's proper clothes.

"We carried your bed here while you slept," grinned Picklepot. "Then we set up the other tricks."

"They're not funny when someone plays them on you, are they?" said Echo sternly.

PLAYFUL

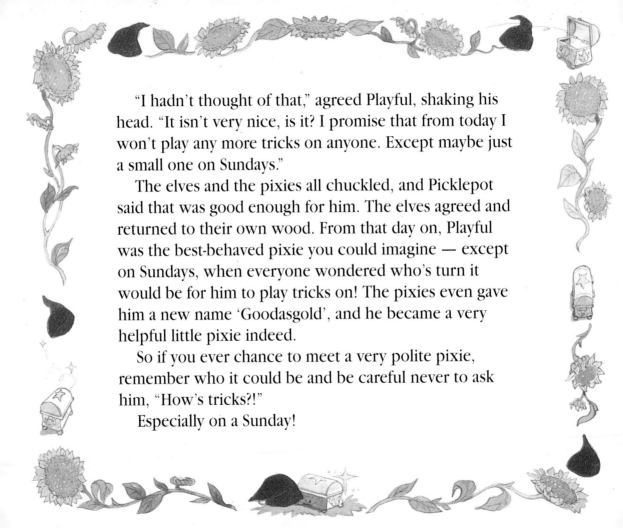

"I hadn't thought of that," agreed Playful, shaking his head. "It isn't very nice, is it? I promise that from today I won't play any more tricks on anyone. Except maybe just a small one on Sundays."

The elves and the pixies all chuckled, and Picklepot said that was good enough for him. The elves agreed and returned to their own wood. From that day on, Playful was the best-behaved pixie you could imagine — except on Sundays, when everyone wondered who's turn it would be for him to play tricks on! The pixies even gave him a new name 'Goodasgold', and he became a very helpful little pixie indeed.

So if you ever chance to meet a very polite pixie, remember who it could be and be careful never to ask him, "How's tricks?!"

Especially on a Sunday!

TRADING PLACES

WRITTEN BY AMBER HUNT

Katina hated being a pixie. Her parents said it was a pixie's job to look after the woodland they lived in, but Katina thought that was boring. What she really wanted to be was a Tooth Fairy and to dress in beautiful fairy clothes and carry a wand, some fairy dust, and the special Tooth Fairy bag. But Katina was a pixie, so she wiped the dew off the grass and polished the leaves and painted and scented the flowers and all the time she was fed up, bored and grumpy.

51

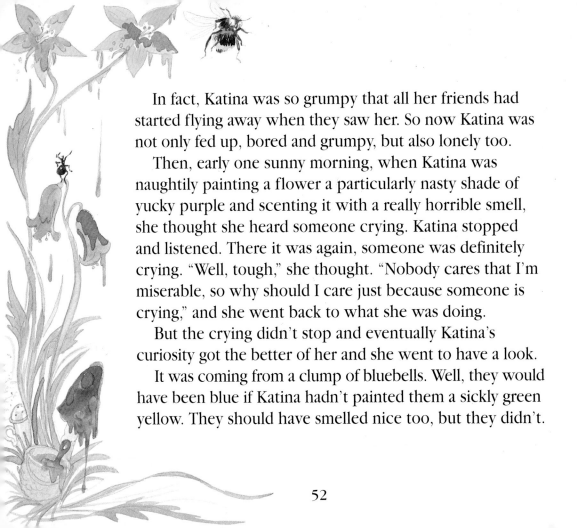

In fact, Katina was so grumpy that all her friends had started flying away when they saw her. So now Katina was not only fed up, bored and grumpy, but also lonely too.

Then, early one sunny morning, when Katina was naughtily painting a flower a particularly nasty shade of yucky purple and scenting it with a really horrible smell, she thought she heard someone crying. Katina stopped and listened. There it was again, someone was definitely crying. "Well, tough," she thought. "Nobody cares that I'm miserable, so why should I care just because someone is crying," and she went back to what she was doing.

But the crying didn't stop and eventually Katina's curiosity got the better of her and she went to have a look.

It was coming from a clump of bluebells. Well, they would have been blue if Katina hadn't painted them a sickly green yellow. They should have smelled nice too, but they didn't.

Katina tip-toed up to the smelly clump of greeny-yellow bells and peeped through. There behind them was … a Tooth Fairy!

"Gosh," said Katina. "A Tooth Fairy! Why are you crying?"

"Because I'm upset, stupid," snapped the Tooth Fairy.

"Oh well, fine," said Katina, "if that's how you feel, you can jolly well go on crying," and she went to fly off.

"No wait," said the fairy. "I'm sorry, I'm not usually rude. It's just that I've sprained my wing and I can't fly." Turning round she showed Katina her hurt wing.

"Oh," said Katina. "What are you going to do?"

"I don't know," sniffed the fairy. "I'm supposed to be visiting a little girl and we never let children down. But there's only a short time left before the little girl wakes up. She'll be so disappointed if her tooth is still there and there's no coin." The fairy started crying again.

"Oh, for goodness sake," said Katina. "Do stop. I'll take you to see my mum and dad. I expect they'll know what to do."

Katina helped the fairy out of the greeny-yellow bells. "What's that horrid smell?" asked the fairy. "And why are those flowers such a revolting colour?"

"Oh, a naughty pixie did that," explained Katina.

"Dreadful," said the fairy. "I hope you don't do things like that." She gave Katina a long hard stare .

As they walked along, Katina suddenly stopped in her tracks. "I've got an idea," she gasped, amazed at her own daring. "I can fly, so why don't I take the coin to the little girl for you and bring you back her tooth? Please let me," she begged.

The fairy looked at Katina thoughtfully, "All right," she said eventually. "There isn't much time though, and you must do exactly as I say."

She gave Katina precise instructions and made Katina repeat them back to her three times before she was satisfied. Finally, she gave Katina the special Tooth Fairy bag and sent her on her way.

Katina flew through the woodland bursting with joy. If she did this well, perhaps she would be allowed to become a Tooth Fairy one day.

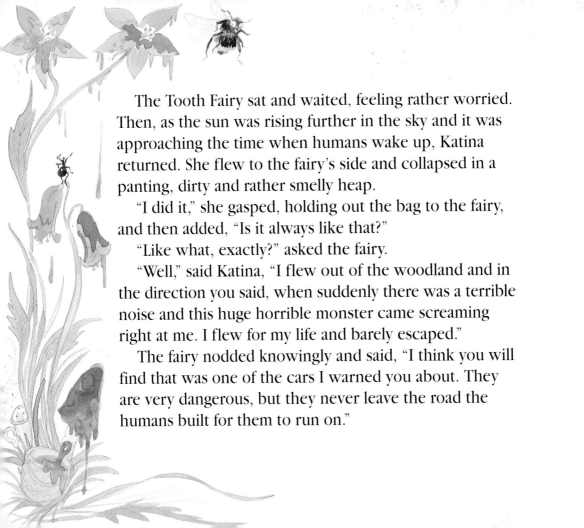

The Tooth Fairy sat and waited, feeling rather worried. Then, as the sun was rising further in the sky and it was approaching the time when humans wake up, Katina returned. She flew to the fairy's side and collapsed in a panting, dirty and rather smelly heap.

"I did it," she gasped, holding out the bag to the fairy, and then added, "Is it always like that?"

"Like what, exactly?" asked the fairy.

"Well," said Katina, "I flew out of the woodland and in the direction you said, when suddenly there was a terrible noise and this huge horrible monster came screaming right at me. I flew for my life and barely escaped."

The fairy nodded knowingly and said, "I think you will find that was one of the cars I warned you about. They are very dangerous, but they never leave the road the humans built for them to run on."

"Oh," said Katina, impressed by the fairy's knowledge. "Then I was chased by a big hairy monster with enormous eyes, massive fangs and hot evil smelling breath."

The fairy laughed.

"That was a dog. They are friendly and mostly they just want to play, but you have to be careful that you don't accidentally get squashed by them."

"After that," went on Katina, "I was chased by another, smaller monster. This one had big green eyes, sharp teeth and claws and it hissed at me. I had to hide in a smelly hill near the little girl's house, until it went away."

"Ah," sighed the fairy, "that was a cat. You have to be careful with cats. Sometimes they just want to play, but sometimes they can be very spiteful. You were wise to hide, although I suspect that what you hid in was called a compost heap. You really do smell quite unpleasant you know."

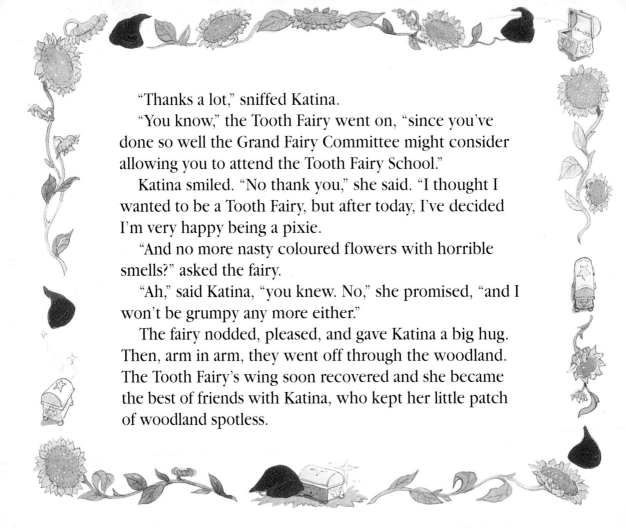

"Thanks a lot," sniffed Katina.

"You know," the Tooth Fairy went on, "since you've done so well the Grand Fairy Committee might consider allowing you to attend the Tooth Fairy School."

Katina smiled. "No thank you," she said. "I thought I wanted to be a Tooth Fairy, but after today, I've decided I'm very happy being a pixie.

"And no more nasty coloured flowers with horrible smells?" asked the fairy.

"Ah," said Katina, "you knew. No," she promised, "and I won't be grumpy any more either."

The fairy nodded, pleased, and gave Katina a big hug. Then, arm in arm, they went off through the woodland. The Tooth Fairy's wing soon recovered and she became the best of friends with Katina, who kept her little patch of woodland spotless.